THE MYSTERIOUS AMAZON RIVER DOLPHIN

By Carol M. Elliott

Scott Foresman
is an imprint of

Glenview, Illinois • Boston, Massachusetts • Chandler, Arizona •
Upper Saddle River, New Jersey

Illustrations

5, 8 Judith Hunt.

Photographs

Every effort has been made to secure permission and provide appropriate credit for photographic material. The publisher deeply regrets any omission and pledges to correct errors called to its attention in subsequent editions.

Unless otherwise acknowledged, all photographs are the property of Pearson Education, Inc.

Photo locators denoted as follows: Top (T), Center (C), Bottom (B), Left (L), Right (R), Background (Bkgd)

Opener: (Inset) ©Mark Carwardine/Nature Picture Library; **1** ©Leonide Principe/ Alamy Images; **3** ©Stockxpert; **4** ©Leonide Principe/Alamy Images; **6** (TL) ©Ablestock/ Alamy, ©Ablestock/Corbis, (Bkgd) ©Wolfgang Kaehler/Alamy Images; **10** (Bkgd) FAN travelstock/Alamy Images; **11** (Inset) ©Mark Carwardine/Nature Picture Library; **12** ©Blaine Harrington III/Alamy Images.

ISBN 13: 978-0-328-46915-4
ISBN 10:   0-328-46915-7

3 4 5 6 7 8 9 10 V010 13 12 11 10

This is the Amazon River. It's the biggest river in South America. All kinds of mammals, birds, and fish live in the Amazon or near it. One of the mammals is bright pink!

This is the boto, or Amazon river dolphin. Most dolphins live in salt water. But the boto lives in fresh water.

Most dolphins have a tall fin on their backs. But the boto has a low ridgelike fin.

A boto breathes air through a blowhole. It's about the same size as other dolphins. It eats fish as other dolphins do.

boto

gray dolphin

It's very hard to study the boto. Dangerous animals live in the Amazon River. Some of these animals can kill people.

piranha

bushmaster snake

The river's water is very dark. The boto can stay under the dark water where people can't see it. It can hold its breath for a long time. That also makes the boto hard to study.

How does the boto find its way in the dark water? It uses echolocation. This means it makes sounds that bounce off things in front of it.

The sound waves echo back to the boto. They make a picture in the dolphin's mind. This means the boto can "see" a tasty fish. Or it can "see" a dangerous enemy.

Have you been to a show like this? Saltwater dolphins can live in tanks. People enjoy watching them. Scientists can learn a lot about them.

But freshwater dolphins are different. Most of them will die if they are kept in a tank. So scientists have to study them in their real home.

How many botos are there? How long does a boto live? We don't know for sure!

Today, the botos need your help. The Amazon River is changing fast. Every year, it gets a little dirtier.

Will the botos be able to stay in their home? Someday, maybe you'll study them and find out!

Amazon Rainforest display
Audubon Aquarium of the Americas
New Orleans, Louisiana